SHADOW EVIDENCE INTELLIGENCE

Shadow Evidence Intelligence
And other formal disruptions

Kristin Prevallet

FACTORY SCHOOL
2006

Acknowledgments

My thanks to the editors of the following presses who published these poems:
- Apostrophe. *Whitman Hom(m)age 2005/1885* (Nantes, France: joca seria press, 2005). Thank you Olivier Brossard and Éric Athenot.
- Amateur Order. *Wherever We Put Our Hats* (#3, March 2006). Thank you Jon Leon.
- Shadow Evidence Intelligence. *Sleeping Fish* (#0.75). Thank you Derek White.
- Oil Oil Oil. *The Brooklyn Rail* (Winter 2003). Thank you Mónica de la Torre.
- Pop-prop agit. *Damn the Caesars* (#2). Thank you Richard Owens and Roger Snell.
- Spear Britney. *Conundrum* (#2). Thank you Kerri Sonnenberg.
- Documentation from the PIPA Archive. *Chain* (#11: Public Forms) Thank you Jena Osman and Juliana Spahr.
- Lexicons: Normalcy, *A.bacus*. Thank you Dan Featherston; Force, *Enough!* Thank you Leslie Scalapino; BoogCity (#2). Thank you David Kirschenbaum.
- The Economy of Poetry. Part one appears in my book, *Scratch Sides: Poetry, Documentation and Image-Text Projects*. Part two appears in *Pierogi Press* (Mark Lombardi Issue) and in the online journal, *Not Enough Night*. Thank you Dale Smith, Susan Swensen, Junior Burke, and Maureen Owen.

Cover image: Jane Fine. Battlefield II, 2003, acrylic and ink on wood, 42″ x 57″. Courtesy of the artist and Pierogi gallery.

Production Assistants: Octavia Davis, J.R. Osborn

Shadow Evidence Intelligence, Kristin Prevallet
First Edition, Factory School 2006
Heretical Texts: Volume 2, Number 3
Series Editor: Bill Marsh

ISBN 1-60001-047-4

factoryschool.org

Making gestures into a void. How long is the effect of a poem-gesture? Mirrors upon mirrors worlds upon worlds – talking, fucking, dying. This to this to this. Rage upon rage. Violence upon violence.

Anne Waldman, from *Vow To Poetry*

Contents

I. SHADOW POEMS: *(Dis)Hommage to Form*

Apostrophe
      (in the shadow of Whitman's "Apostrophe")   *13*

Amateur Order
      (in the shadow of Stevens' "Connoisseur of Chaos")   *16*

Shadow Evidence Intelligence
      (in the shadow of Colin Powell)   *23*

Cruelty and Conquest
      (in the shadow of George Bush)   *26*

Jack
      (in the shadow of Mother Goose)   *30*

II. CONCEPTUAL POETICS: *Formal Disruptions*

Pop-Prop-Agit   *35*

Documents from the PIPA (Poetry Is Public Art) Archive   *47*

The Economy of Poetry   *65*

Appendix   *73*

For Sophie –

"There are W's everywhere!"

SHADOW POEMS: *(Dis)Hommage to Form*

Apostroph
(in the shadow of Whitman's "Apostroph")

O daughter! O me!

O international agencies!

O mountain lilacs of my mountainous youth!

O cosmic strings! O cheap labor!

O urban sprawl! O chaos of dictators!

O hopeless future! O soulmate!

O internal source! O longevity!

O fear! O God *in absentia*! O moral norm.

O poets! O goateed carpenters! O street slumberers!

O ignorance! The cold sparrow's window song! Even in winter, she
wakes up early.

O, as I walk riverside, I see the darkening clouds — the devilish
shapes, pink and gray, through the sunset ...

O I saw and still see, triggered thunder; O soldiers! See how they
control even the sky!

O animal warning, unheeded! (Silence them, before they learn to
speak!)

O cynicism! Middle ground! (O if the whole world knows injustice,
why don't they rebel?)

O I believe there is nothing pure about America and her freedom!

O impostors! Interlopers! Invaders! Thieves! How mighty the fanatics
have become!

O you who dare to represent us and them!

O self-adorned king! O southern trees bearing noose marks, still!

O to occupy through grace! O generosity!

O all of us, separable — time, time, time!

*O CURSE HE THAT WOULD DISSEVER THIS UNION FOR ANY
REASON WHATEVER!*

O evil, o slaughter, o giant wave!

O torture exported to the highest bidder!

O fear shapers, O bomb threats! O celebrated terrorist!

O suburbs, O the slum! The citizens are shopping their minds away.

O utopia where everyone gets stared at equally!

O fake Louis Vuitton! Fake pashima! Did he who made the lamb,
make thee?

O child's hand in Indochina!

O images of future centuries! O dreams of a better world!

O strength and luck, don't leave me now!

O hour of my need!

O workmen building the structures which sustain me!

O immigrant laborers nailing boards for 15 hours straight!

O subway drivers! Cab drivers! We travel together every day!

O I will make the encyclopedia of all your lost and forgotten
glimpses!

O internal conflict! I love and I hate you, always!

O storage of childhood junk! O inseparable toy bunny!

O sun, o moon! Move along, you know nothing different.

O brooder! O I must start building my own life, before we all die!

O biodiversity! O organic farmers! I won't speak for you, but I'll buy
your apples.

O poisonous river, my neighbor!

O rigged contests, O privatization! I can't save you, I'm not your poet!

O goodbye past decades! Feminists! Nuns! Public mourners!

O courage of rainbow people!

O vast preparations for emancipation! Black and white! O diversity,
they now call you dogma.

O how long does it take for a message to reach the future! What will
they say when they see what we have become!

O clairvoyants! O teachers! To separate morality from judgment.

O reality! Filter down, filter down, to all red states!

O Birthday! O Jesus! O humble adoration, unlegislated faith.

O conviction! Infect troops of poets! Artists! Singers!

O depression! O unproductive passionate intensity!

O songs of freedom! Songs of contractor, middleman, manager,
sergeant!

O arrogance! O freedom! What's being done in your name, to your
seekers?

O ecstatic liars!

O me, I, they! Preparing for what? Afraid of what?

O insurgency! O dark ages! O phoenix inspire oppressors and
oppressed to rise above their worst inclinations!

O brilliant, burning, amazing youth!

O visionary slogan-makers, still writing dissent on subway walls!

O prophets! You started writing self-help books and lost what was
most inarticulate about your vision!

O unspoken! O cosmic and biological marriage! O consciousness! O
quark!

O America, you have been dissevered!

O Whitman, who never saw it coming!

O my soul! O powerless speech!

O infant, speck on the century!

O states! Cities! Buying conformity over human rights! I can't love
you as you self-destruct.

O death wish! Why else would they vote for terminators!

O new history! Forge inarticulatable humanity! Scratches! Scratches!
Push forward into speech!

O muted poets! O you sitting there! What are you hearing in this
broad dribble?

O height I seek! O infinity in an empty bowl!

O nameless force! Threatening apocalypse by making it happen!

O sculpted history! They pull a lever and you quake!

O unseasonably warm sea, glaciers drop like fallen towers!

O poets, the sick fish and the floating limbs! All counting on you!

Amateur Order
(in the shadow of Stevens' "Connoisseur of Chaos")

I.

A.   The end
is an explosion.

B.   The beginning
is an explosion.

C.   (Pages of Illustrations.)
1. A soldier firing at a man who is
firing at him, both are hit,
both are falling.
2. Oil pooling into the crevices and
holes at the center of the earth.
3. A falling man memorizes a soldier
face just as he pulls the trigger. At
the center of the earth, a volcano.

II.

If its all about oil,
>   and it is.
If poppies are growing wild again in the hills of Afghanistan,
>   and they are.
If the butchers of Baghdad past and the butchers of Baghdad present
are the past and present butchers of Baghdad,
>   and they are.
If America was fooled to believe that a country decimated by
sanctions and bombed to pieces for 12 long years was somehow in
possession of weapons capable of eliminating the free world,
>   and we were.
If hundreds of thousands have been killed, wounded, maimed, gone
crazy, committed suicide just in the past year and just because of war,
>   and they have.
If the memory of 9/11 is the tigers leap into the future and the future
is the present ruled by madmen,
>   and it is.
If terrorism is a many-headed hydra fueled by hatred and aggression, if
fundamentalists are fueled by hatred and aggression, if their side and
our side and all sides who think in terms of good and evil are fueled
by hatred and aggression,
>   and it is, and they are, and we are.
If most corporations work to undermine the interests of the people
and political conventions are funded by corporations,
>   and they are.
If the origin of oil is inorganic and comes from the magma centermost
layer of the earth,
>   and it may be, perhaps.
If ideas like viruses spread from mind to mind, if culture evolves
through the spread of ideas, if ideas can be poisioned, manipulated,
spun out of control,
>   and they can.
If cluster bombs spread shrapnel indiscriminately to enter bodies and
explode into tiny bits, if bombs are only as precise as the eye of the
trigger, if the eye of the trigger is human,
>   and it is.
If the morals of a society can be judged by the way it treats its
prisoners, if 33 counties in the U.S. currently have 60% of their
population in jail,
>   and they do
>   and it can
>   and it is true

If I am a person wanting only to be conscious,
If consciousness is as lethal as a full metal jacket,
If the still point of the turning wheel sucks chaos into itself
      and becomes sickened,
      off course,
      insane,
      ludicrous,
            and I am
            and we are
            and it is
            and it is

If silence felled the tree because the fall landed on deaf ears,
If an evil man is a man who lacks a conscious and a truly evil man is
one who believes his empty conscious is righteous, holy, and good,
      then .... and it has.... and he is .... and they are
            the trees
            the torture
            the future
            the memory
            the bombs
            the dead
            the point.

III.

When the contrast between life and death is made ugly
by the fact of so many people dying ugly deaths,
When all the beautiful ideas
about how life and death are one
seem so privileged,
Lucky the few
who are allowed to live out
their natural lives
without being blown
to pieces.
Life and death,
a twinned horned monster
that eats its tail and
gags
bulges
explodes.

If a soldier dies while maiming
another person the last
living memory of that soldier's life
will be in the mind of the
person maimed;
so the last memory of you
is in the mind of the
people who behold you
so be gentle with them lest
they be gentle with your image
in memory
in mourning
in the work of
seeing you in life.
Memory survives
the corporal state:
this is the only afterlife you can be sure of.

Isn't this a good enough reason
to resist joining in the logic
of an imperial army?

IV.

A. Well, a new order certainly is a violent one.
This proves something. A new order is predicated on lies.
A truth in the otherwise distorted, maimed, tortured flow of information.
News.
Everyone has their own version of the facts.
In the streamline.
In the flow.
In the wires.
Just one more spinner
on the lake, on the immense
disorder of truths.

B. It is June while I write.
Somehow there is a chill in the air.
Bone shivering. Hacking. Feverish.
Summer will be hot as hell, it will come to this,
a change in the weather a change in the bile.
Keel over
Die biking
Die watching sports
Die bombing
Die bad heart
Die liars
Die presidential authority, presidential atrocity
Regal burials for former presidents who are murderers.

The violence of the new order strikes
itself in the face
and implodes.
Did you hear,
have you heard
the news?

B and C are not fixed in time and place.
They're not posing for some eternal portrait,
their winter has been a long cold reign
but they are nothing more than stick men
chalked on the sidewalk.
It does not take much pensiveness
to see that
the people stomping

on the figures
are smearing away
the images one by one:
they are resigning
coming clean
resisting
because their morals
are no more permanent
than chalk.

V.

The stomping crowds:
they perceive the mountain
which seems so unmovable
to be an oyster
in disguise.
They kick it
squash it
return it to the sea.
Poor evil oyster
mistook the entirety of the earth
and all the conflicting systems therein
to be his bed....

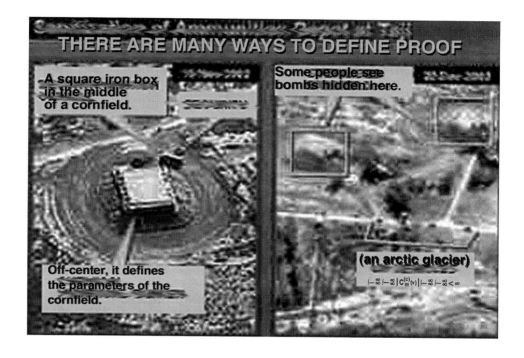

For example, people stand in different places and see the same thing, but at a different speed

25 Nov 2002

Cylinders maximally separated in space

Tubes neutron in their projected motion

There are fish, the size of infinity

DON'T LET THEM SEE THIS.

There are crows the size of crows

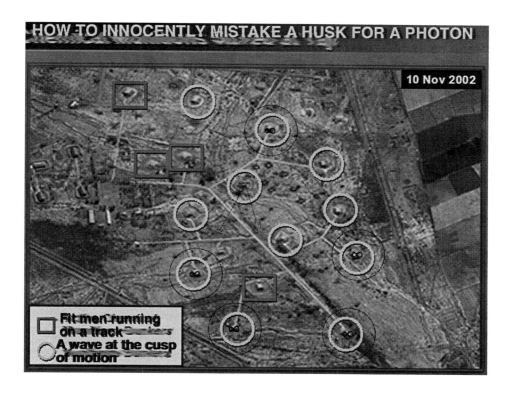

Cruelty and Conquest

VII.
The United States has no
quarrel with the Iraqi people;
they've suffered too
long in silent
captivity. Liberty for
the Iraqi people is
a great moral cause, and a great strategic
goal. The people
of Iraq deserve
it; the security of
all nations requires it. Free societies do not
intimidate through cruelty
and conquest, and
open societies do not
threaten the world with mass murder. The United
States supports political
and economic liberty
in a unified Iraq.
(George Bush to the United Nations, September 2002)

VI.
The United States has no
quarrel oil the Iraqi people; they've suffered too
oil in silent
captivity. Liberty for
the oil people is
a great moral cause, oil a great strategic
goal. The people
oil Iraq deserve
it; the security of
oil nations requires it. Free societies do oil
intimidate through cruelty
and conquest, and
oil societies do not
threaten the world oil mass murder. The United
States supports oil
and economic liberty
in a unified oil.

V.

The United States has no
oil oil the Iraqi people; they've oil too
oil in silent
captivity. Oil for
the oil people is
oil great moral cause, oil a oil strategic
goal. The people
oil oil deserve
it; the security of
oil nations requires it. Free societies oil oil
intimidate through cruelty
and oil, and
oil societies do not
oil the world oil mass murder. Oil United
States supports oil
and oil liberty
in a unified oil.

IV.

The United States oil no
oil oil the oil people; they've oil too
oil in silent
captivity. Oil oil
the oil people is
oil great moral cause, oil oil oil strategic
goal. The oil
oil oil deserve
it; oil security of
oil nations oil it. Free societies oil oil
intimidate through cruelty
and oil, and
oil societies do oil
oil the world oil oil murder. Oil United
States oil oil
and oil liberty
oil a unified oil.

27

III.
Oil United States oil oil
oil oil the oil people; they've oil oil
oil in silent
oil. Oil oil
the oil people is
oil oil moral cause, oil oil oil strategic
goal. Oil oil
oil oil oil
it; oil security of
oil nations oil oil. Free societies oil oil
intimidate through cruelty
oil oil, and
oil oil do oil
oil oil world oil oil oil. Oil United
States oil oil
and oil oil
oil a unified oil.

II.
Oil United Oil oil oil
oil oil the oil people; they've oil oil
oil oil silent
oil. Oil oil
the oil people is
oil oil moral oil, oil oil oil strategic
goal. Oil oil
oil oil oil
it; oil security of
oil nations oil oil. Free societies oil oil
intimidate oil cruelty
oil oil, and
oil oil do oil
oil oil world oil oil oil. Oil United
States oil oil
and oil oil
oil oil unified oil.

I.

Oil Oil Oil oil oil
oil oil oil oil oil; they've oil oil
oil oil oil
oil. Oil oil
the oil oil is
oil oil oil oil, oil oil oil strategic
oil. Oil oil
oil oil oil
oil; oil oil of
oil nations oil oil. Oil societies oil oil
oil oil oil
oil oil, and
oil oil oil oil
oil oil oil oil oil oil. Oil United
Oil oil oil
and oil oil
oil oil oil oil.

Jack

This is the dream that scared George.

This is the crab
That starred in the dream that scared George.

This is the bag
That chased the crab
That starred in the dream that scared George.

This is the wind
That blew the bag
That chased the crab
That starred in the dream that scared George.

This is the cloud
That made the wind
That blew the bag
That chased the crab
That starred in the dream that scared George.

This is the plane with the silver tip
That bombed through the cloud
That made the wind
That blew the bag
That chased the crab
That starred in the dream that scared George.

This is the pilot, totally ripped
That steered the plane with the silver tip
That bombed through the cloud
That made the wind
That blew the bag
That chased the crab
That starred in the dream that scared George.

This is the mosque all rubbled and torn
Bulls eye to the pilot, totally ripped
That steered the plane with the silver tip
That bombed through the cloud
That made the wind
That blew the bag

That chased the crab
That starred in the dream that scared George.

This is the boy, now all alone,
That cleans his gun with a femur bone
That he found in the mosque all shattered and torn
Bulls eye to the pilot, totally ripped
That steered the plane with the silver tip
That bombed through the cloud
That made the wind
That blew the bag
That chased the crab
That starred in the dream that scared George.

This is the sea that recedes at night
That shelters the boy, now all alone
That cleans his gun with a femur bone
That he found in the mosque all shattered and torn
Bulls eye to the pilot, totally ripped
That steered the plane with the silver tip
That bombed through the cloud
That made the wind
That blew the bag
That chased the crab
That starred in the dream that scared George.

This is the war that from far away
Made the ocean step back from the shore that day
And a lonely crab all battered and worn
Laid down in the sand and died there —
Until the bag
and the wind
and the cloud
and the plane
and the pilot
and the house
and the boy
and the bone
came to George in a dream
          and it's dreams
                    that scare kings
                         because a dream
                                   makes the   king

see the   seams
                                of his logic
            unravel into the
                        babble
                                    of his true
            state of mind:
                        I N S A N E

CONCEPTUAL POETICS: *Formal Disruptions*

Pop-Prop-Agit

SPECIAL DESCRIPTION
· The following fragments are filed under Special File
(sf)230 as "pop-prop-agit."
· Human profiles indicate attempt to directly counter The
Official Administration by never calling "it" by name.
· The following are inscriptions written on subway walls
after the attacks of September, June, July, October, and
May; of the interminable years following 2001 respectively,
up to the present which is currently defined as two years
later, five years later, 15 years later; this being after the
third interminable war which futurists looking back describe
as "the poly-lateral unmediated mutual-nuclear strike."
· The subway being no longer identified as such.
· The inscriptions are not signed, but here are organized by
personality profile and handwriting analysis and logged under
the following designations: M1, Ltt20, KayVe23, MiaLoy30,
WanWi21.
· There are photograph fragments left over from layers of
subway advertisements upon which these inscriptions occur
and these appear as [photofrag + descript] in the log.
· The inscriptions amount to no said "person"; no said
"person" is data listed in the records held by the Bureau of
Public Disturbance.
· Hereafter called "Covert Operation x2500intact" and
"c240sync."
· Inscribers may have used a singular female of unknown
origin to track their progression through the tunnels.
· Certain slogans appear to contradict the Official
Administration's Kill Dissent Operation, although because
they are written in covert "poetic speak" do not seem to be
overtly political.
· Here they are transcribed as "full sentence" (fs) or
"fragment" (fg). If "fragment" (fg) then pieces are spliced
together using the assumed logic of the coverts.

· Key:
      f/s = fragment, spliced [phonetic = fsss]
      f/g = fragment, no splice [phonetic = fggg]
      w/s = whole sentence [phonetic = wsss]
      o/n = official note [phonetic = ooom]

POP-PROP-AGIT FILE #1: M1

PsychProfile= central ego intact. Mind for complexity, nuance.
Suspect for FAD (Future Acts of Defiance).

War is the pursuit (f/s) of an ideal world imagined (f/s) by (f/s) who
    has the biggest weapons
w/s= The first directive is to impose an image of the imagined world onto
    the population
w/s= Propaganda is an advertisement that sells war and in turn sells the
    image of an ideal world o/n=*in 2010, this famous slogan became an advertisement for*
    Volkswagen
f/g= Live in Los Vegas
Simultaneously on the TV (f/s) the constant replay of falling towers
f/g= Simultaneously along the "G" and "L" lines
f/g= PRONOUNCE
w/s= Is "she" elvis? o/n=*reference to possible sighting?*
f/g= Not just that
This photograph is (f/s) inhuman war

POP-PROP-AGIT FILE #2: LTT20

Psych Profile=Central ego disattached. Confused identity, vague,
laments the "past." Probably PSP (Probable Suicide Potential).

w/s= I love Britney
w/s= She has absorbed the anger, fear, confusion
The flags (f/s) corner symbol of Am (o/n=*short for American*) Dream (f/s) no
    longer possible
w/s= A taunting reminder of how things used to be
I will not (f/s) "return to normal"
Her face (f/s) backwards normalcy
w/s= They had some displaced aggression
w/s= Yea, as if
Take it out (f/s) against the image
The event is already (f/s) saturated, over-represented
w/s= Displaced aggression against it
It was not the isolated (f/s) event of these photos
w/s= What can be separated from my immediate fear?
Pop (f/s) star super freak
w/s= Always the possibility
Mask society writes (f/s) its own meaning. o/n=*reference to 20thc philos. Barthes*
Her androgyny (f/s) slate
f/g= Punish

POP-PROP-AGIT #3: KayVe23

Psych Profile=central ego intact. Writes in DM (Dialogic Mode).
Possibly suspect for F.A.D. (Future Acts of Defiance). Tendencies
towards probable logic (a.k.a. fantasy, irrational desires.)

w/s= Why is her chest flat?
w/s= Don't let this happen to your little girl
w/s= Fuck me please
w/s= One more time
w/s= She is not fake
w/s= Don't believe the hype
w/s= Anyone can be a star
w/s= ~~Stop~~ Start Rape Culture. o/n: *Something is written by one person that is then crossed out by another.*
The stain upon which reality revolves (f/s) into the real (f/s) the mysterious detail
f/g= sticks it out
f/g= 'Fit' into the symbolic network
Of reality as such (f/s) "something is amiss" o/n: *reference to 20thc philos. Slavoj Zizek.*

POP-PROP-AGIT #4: MiaLoy30

Psych Profile=central ego disattached. Clear-headed, but angry;
prolific. Seems to be leaving instructions for other inscribers to
follow. Overuses maxims as rhetorical strategy.

w/s= I have an awareness of needing to move beyond
The image and into the (f/s) intention behind it. Why is it here?
w/s= I am not accidental
w/s= Displaced aggression o/n=*seems to be in dialogue with LTT20*
w/s= who is powerful?
Defacement (f/s) symbolic intent misguided
Analyzing the image (f/s) do not avoid the politics (f/s) behind the
    defacement
f/g= A sign is made
Light obliterates the ability (f/s) to think outside of it
All of us are suspect (f/s) at some level
This defacement is (f/s) not a symbolic gesture (f/s) it is an act of
    dissent
I displace my anger away (f/s) from the actual source (f/s) of power that
    is causing (f/s) me the pain, directed (f/s) against other objects—
    creating signs (f/s) codes (f/s) out of the things themselves (f/s)
    that then point to a larger critique o/n=*this is the longest inscription found so far on*
    the subway walls, coordinates x30, y65
When in fascism (f/s) any critique of government (f/s) is considered
    suspect (f/s) critique is displaced
w/s= Do not try to directly confront, but move around
w/s= Come at it from a different angle that is still pointed
f/g= But not immediately recognizable
The face of woman (f/s) bound and gagged (f/s) fucked and cut open
    (f/s) all the possible acts (f/s) of violence that can (f/s) be done to a
    woman (f/s) in times of war.
o/n= *this refers to subway advertisements of Britney Spears, defaced after Sept 11, 2001, G-train,*
    Brooklyn. These images, preserved in our databases, are intact. See Photofrag File G240A, below
w/s= Crime rates are down but crimes against women are up
w/s= What is on the rise?
w/s= checkcheck regime is largely financed by powerful military-industrial
    complex and wealthy big business checkcheck regime is xenophobic and
    propaganda-obsessed checkcheck w/s= "Homeland/Fatherland" glorified
    checkcheck
w/s= Wake up

POP-PROP-AGIT #5: WanWi21

Psych Profile=confused, a copycat, the least interesting of the inscribers; could be A.B.D. (Already Born Dead). Writes one-liners, inside jokes. Doesn't seem concerned about accessibility.

w/s= ferocious displaced competition

w/s= replicate the sacrifice of labor

w/s= between parallel sides, the heart

w/s= fascinating disarray

w/s= recognize utopia

w/s= promote abstract culture

w/s= words drove abstractionism

w/s= double locus art

w/s= "just wars"

w/s= identify universal damage

w/s= sin is all too natural

fluid material can be articulated (f/s) (but only war)

w/s= blinded, brutal, symbolic

w/s= intervention of justice

w/s= alarm moral police

moral intervention: (f/s) a process of armed repression (f/s) rooted in a
    police mentality

w/s= extreme fury

attack form: (f/s) the emergence dictates (f/s) the terms and nature of the
    transformation

w/s= hint of the struggles that will move modern limits

w/s= real threats, creative shifts

w/s= endanger ourselves as private and solitary

w/s= the choice of the future is whether to buy and consume anything at all

w/s= swallow up the entire cosmos

w/s= replace one pious multiplex

w/s= where you are nowhere

w/s= you are, are you?

POP-PROP-AGIT #6: Supplemental

Poster designed and wheatpasted, spread throughout subway tunnels
to agitate passersby. Probably collaboration between KayVe and
MiaLoy30. Ineffective as P.M.T. (Political Anti-machinary Tactic).
Annoying as anti-everything.

+++

A SITUATION

WAR IS THE PURSUIT OF AN IDEAL WORLD IMAGINED BY
WHO HAS THE BIGGEST WEAPONS.
THE FIRST DIRECTIVE: TO IMPOSE AN IMAGE OF THE IMAGINED WORLD
ONTO THE POPULATION.
PROPAGANDA IS AN ADVERTISEMENT THAT SELLS WAR AND IN TURN
SELLS THE IMAGE OF AN IDEAL WORLD.
SIMULTANEOUSLY ON THE TV, THE CONSTANT REPLAY OF
FALLING TOWERS.
REMEMBER WHEN WE HADN'T YET BEEN TOLD TO
"RETURN TO NORMAL?"

+++

POP-PROP-AGIT #7: Spear Britney (Photofrag File G240A)

the future
choice is
whether to buy
and consume
anything at all

START
STOP
RAPE
CULTURE

smother
one pious
multiplex

articulate fluid material

MISDIRECTED SYMBOLIC INTENT

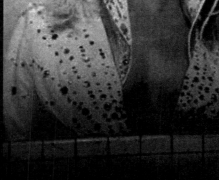

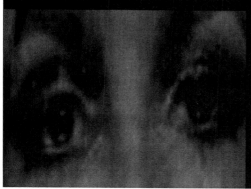

No image obliterates the ability to think outside of it.

Reality Revolves upon a Stain

between parallel sides, there is a heart

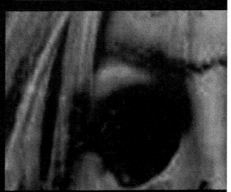

Is "she" Elvis or is this war?

Documentation From The PIPA (Poetry Is Public Art) Project Archives

The PIPA (Poetry Is Public Art) Project is a conceptual collaborative endeavor based on the site-specific potential of poetry projects to intersect with public spaces. What this means is that poetry can happen anywhere, at any time. It can intersect with space and time not as random wordplay but as covert reflective commentary. PIPA is a concept that has been exorcised around the world for many centuries. PIPA has no members except for those who, intentionally or non-intentionally, choose to break poetry out of the frame of the page and test its assimilation and/or intrusion into public spaces. Although the archive implies organization, there is no organizing principle behind PIPA, except for the organizing principles at work in the mind of any poet who, at any time, chooses to design, orate, sloganize, decorate, or sculpturally infiltrate public space. (*See disclaimer.*) PIPA is not a container for the minds of poets, but rather is a convergence of minds working independently or in groups to infiltrate public spaces at the level of poetry. PIPA activities will include and/or have included:

- any poetry activity that causes passersby to pause
- handing out poems on busy avenues (the haughtier the better)
- slapping poetry stickers on advertisements that "talk back" to the advertisement
- leaving poems behind on park or subway benches (which brings up the problematic poetics of littering)
- leaving poems in the form of messages on phone booths or public toilets that cause passersby to pause and think: that language looks quite strange
- writing responses on subway and bus advertisements (after all, they are trying to talk to you.)
- proclaiming poetry from soapboxes
- using poets' condensers-of-language skills to create witty and provocative slogans for political rallies
- designing poetry signs to blend in with the surrounding signage
- spray-painting the sidewalk through the ingenious method of stenciling and cutting out slogans at the base of a cardboard box
- etc.

This list from the PIPA archives is not the work of one, but rather many publicly-minded poets. And it is quite possible and even likely that the numerous people involved in the above projects do not know that the PIPA archives are chronicling their activities. PIPA hopes that the poetry practitioners alluded to in this document know the spirit of camaraderie and generosity that is at the heart of PIPA. The PIPA of possibility is equally the PIPA of hazard. The PIPA of enthusiasm is also the PIPA of failure.

Disclaimer: PIPA officially (but not because there are any officials) denies any allegiance to hierarchy or status within the collective but unidentified mind-which-is-PIPA. There are no members as such of PIPA, and no official spokesperson. This documentation is not to be confused with any official statement. Regardless, YOU are PIPA if you choose to participate in the endeavor to create site-specific poetry interventions into public spaces. Often such interventions are against the law. Check with the particular legal apparatus of your state (if you care) before embracing PIPA. (Which is not an ideology, and therefore cannot be embraced. Only manifested.)

Archive #1: The RealPo PIPA Chronicles

In the Fall of 2000, I was a member of the RealPo listserve which facilitated the flow of PIPA. What follows is an excerpt from the correspondence and is used without the permission of the correspondents.

Subject: Re: lines for covert poetry

September 25, 2000

> I am working on imagining how poetry IS public art. There are models in the art world—lets start reporting on these, and collecting our sources.

Mon, 25 Sep 2000

> As for poetry and the public—one of the things I've started doing is handing out "Poetry Cards," sort of. Interesting pieces of art or postcards or whatever with a poem on the back. Of course, most people don't know what they are getting, but if you are in the right place or whatever most people will, just on instinct, take whatever it is you offer. I think because it appeals to their filmic sense of themselves as being the focal point of everything. So they think maybe nothing and they take the cool looking card without even thinking about it (maybe even just to get you to leave them alone, or not talk to them more or something, but let's leave that insecurity unsaid, shall we?) And then of course they look at it, when they see it isn't a flier for like Pizza Towne or something, and they read it, almost whether they want to or not, when they are sitting in their train or waiting for the elevator or whatever. It's sort of a poetics assault—fuck you, I know you don't want poetry, but you need it, and here it is. I got this idea from a project Mike Grinthal did with CD Wright, where he would go around wheat-pasting poems in downtown Providence, where all of the suited fold would have no choice but to see it, day after day. His is more anarchist, and I like it better, and if anyone would want to do that in NY let me know. We've all done this sort of thing—hanging poems from the things you hold onto on the train, on lamps in restaurants, things like that. It's like MDs giving medicine to children, pardon the pretense.

25 Sep 2000

> I have often thought about giving away my poetry, leaflet style, on the streets. But as one who has handed out many a political leaflet

in my high school volunteering for my local state representative days, I have seen what happens to most of those leaflets. While it's lovely to imagine that folks will take these "Poetry Cards" from you and carry them around until finding themselves in a rare instance of having nothing to occupy themselves they look to the leaflet for help, and there find a taste of enlightenment staring them in their previously clouded eyes, in reality they will likely walk to the corner and deposit your beautiful "Poetry Card" in the trash receptacle or just as likely, on the ground. Perhaps I'm being cynical here, but that's what my experience suggests. A suggestion I have is to send poetry as a random e-mail. Just pick a name at random and add @yahoo or @hotmail and likely it'll get there. Poetry in that form is more likely to be read and, even better, more likely to be forwarded on. Plus the obvious fact that it doesn't use paper and you will never have to see your poetry in a trashcan or beneath anonymous loafers.

September 25, 2000

Ok—good points. No poetry as public littering. How about stamping poetry onto those subway advertisements? I like that idea! But lets come up with stamping slogans: everyone contribute a line from one of your poems. Here's mine: We are all aliens, and we have been here all along.

September 25, 2000

here's mine...

please don't eat monkey. Or, throw in some crickets he'll make an omelet. (Actually this will be good for subway people because I heard from a transit worker the other day that a box of monkeys got loose on the L Train and they were hard to catch because they were swinging all over the place, he also told me he found a head in a box and a couple of other really disgusting stories.)

26 Sep 2000

The Bronx zoo already owns the cricket omelet poem. No cheating. I vote for a stamp of Pound's "in the station of the metro." Where do we get these stamps made? I get paid next week.

26 Sep 2000

I was bike-riding on quiet very well-off DC side street last week & someone had chalked in big pink on an uphill one way street:

KIDS
YOUR
EATING
STOP

Wed, 26 Sep 2000

I love the idea of stamping poetry. A few years back some people in California (or maybe elsewhere, too) were stamping "queer money" on dollar bills. Poetry on money, how perfect. Here's a line: nixed as heaven, oh boy, a dagger that tilts left.

Thu, 27 Sep 2000

We could send mass stamped postcards to Governor Bush's camp ... With words something along the lines of: Beetles ... you kill people like beetles; or: Alaska ... State not oilfield. We could also make bumper stickers and sticker everything ... I have a program on my computer that makes bumper stickers and the sticky paper you print it on is really cheap.

Thu, 27 Sep 2000

My PIPA line contribution: snails are beautiful until someone gets hurt.

Wed, 27 Sep 2000

We could make stamps and sneak into newsagents and stamp all the newspapers with the news that isn't fit to print. And we could stamp billboards too. I love the idea of a tiny stamp on a huge ad. We could stamp everything.

The Sydney Harbor Bridge now has official graffiti (temporarily overtaken by Olympic rings). On New Years Eve they lit up a sign that says Eternity. I think it's going back on the bridge after the Olympics. But it was originally graffiti art spray painted all over Sydney by...oh no I've blanked. Will get back with his name. Hmmm.

September 28, 2000

So. In rubber stamp land, each 1/4 inch = one line. One line takes up 9 inches of a stamp. That would be $14.90. A huge stamp! Most stamp pads are only about 2 inches. One line on a two inch stamp costs $5.60. This information comes to us from www.stampsfirst. com. Stamps can be anywhere from 1 line to 20 lines!!! (20 lines, 9 inches, costs about $100. That's the most expensive).

Shall we start a Poetry Is Public Art (PIPA) project? We can place one big order for stamps, and then we can distribute them. Should we stamp with other people's stamps, or our own? Maybe we can all agree to stamp madly on a certain day, no matter where we are.

Warning: stamping may be illegal in some states.

We can also make cards that read Poetry Is Pubic Art with the realpo web address and give them to people if they ask. We should take photographs of a few of our stamps and post them on the web site. This will be PIPA phase one. Then we'll move on to phase two.

September 28, 2000

9-inches of stamp? We could get little roller inkers instead of stamp pads. We could also get self-inking stamps. You can get self-inking stamps with a tray of letters that you actually arrange on the stamp. Kind of like your very own letter-press. We should definitely do Pound's "in a station in the metro" and realpo poems too. The postcard idea is great. We can stamp the postcards. Oh we can even just nick those free postcards from bars and stamp them. I'm into stamping and stealing.

Here's my line: not everyone can have perfect organs

September 27, 2000

Yr story of the monkeys swinging around a subway car has cheered me up immensely. It reminded me of a story about Brooklyn College. One time someone was bringing a box of parrots through for some reason, probably scientific experiments or something, and dropped it, so now parrots live on Brooklyn College campus, squawking at everyone from the trees. Here is my line: When approaching the gates of the unbuildable city...

28 Sep 2000

I think making smart signs for political rallies is a good thing to do. For the anti-bombing rally, we came up with some good ones: "Dear World Bank: Free People Not Markets." Anyway, the few times I've made signs it is amazing how much attention they get in terms of people coming up and talking to you, getting your picture taken, etc. Handing out flyers with poems on them would be interesting in that context. Of course it doesn't have to be so blatantly political—I think the "No More Prisons" stencils that are spray-painted all over the streets of Brooklyn and Manhattan is public art that is also poetry.

28 Sep 2000

Here is my line: all dreams, dreams of waking

28 Sep 2000

Cowboys, Cowgirls, and Cows—

step A- sit on corner

step B- offer strangers dollars (marked or not) to hear your poems and then critique them. Be prepared with extra copies and pencils...

28 September 2000

How about these: phones are ok its just the conversation that scares me; Because of your clothes I'm oppressed; I want to foist my half baked opinions on you; anonymous misanthropic sloganeering for a better America; Clandestine alienation is where it's at; My war with self will be waged on the streets; If I only had a T-shirt company.

29 September 2000

Public Art Ideas: seein' as how no-one's going to do it for me, i've taken to advertising my own poetry w/ magic marker on white wifebeaters. Not as widespread as stamping could be, but at least it's exposure. Perhaps those who live in the bay area should make some and sell them at the Berkeley poetry festival. I just got back from the office supply store and out of impulse and poetry as public art I bought a bunch of magnet sheets that run through my printer. I have been placing poems and images on people's cars. Let me know if anyone wants a magnet to place. The stamps are a great plan.

Conspicuous Consumer On Board; My Other Car Is A Tank; 66% More Likely To Kill You In An Accident; 75% More Likely To Have An Accident; Haulin' Wood. I Swear; Got A Problem With My Bad Ass, Dial 1-800-EAT-SHIT; Am I Driving Poorly? Call Me On My Cell Phone! I would submit any of those to the covert poetry stamp. Or, officially: Nor is your hair more wistful than the western wind. Because didn't people spray paint "O Western Wind" on the Tube when it first got going, whenever that was?

29 September 2000

Cildo Meireles, the Brazilian Artist in the early nineteen seventies, stamped money and coca cola bottles: the bottles were stamped with anti-corporate statements in white so the text was only visible when the glass (recycled) bottles were filled. Bottlers, rather than spilling the product circulated the bottles again and again. Her project was called "insertions into ideological circuits."

29 September 2000

During the gulf war a friend of mine got a red rubber stamp made that said: Government Approved Information & went around to newsstands stamping newspapers with it. I still want to get stickers made that say Thank You for Not Thinking to put on tvs.

Where they are now: Well, small poetry cards were indeed printed and distributed on subways, left on benches (to be cleaned up by MTA janitors), stuck in phone booths, and inserted into advertisements. Magnets with anti-SUV slogans were printed and stuck on SUVs in California and New York. The only effect (but it's not really about the effect, is it?) was one PIPA enfacer [*enfacer* (noun) = a person who leaves behind propaganda, but doesn't deface property] getting yelled at by a SUV owner. But, although the gesture remains a gesture (not a movement) some good PIPA slogans were generated, and did appear on signs at several political rallies, including the Republican convention, the (un)inauguration, and two IMF/World Bank protests.

Here are some of the slogans by RealPo PIPA:
• Dear Bush: Other people exist in the world, too
• Dear Bush: Other life exists in the world and we need it to breathe
• Dear Bush: Arsenic is not a drinkable substance
• Dear Bush: Carbon dioxide, arsenic, lead and benzene are not
    vegetables
• I voted...I think
• Ballot Victim
• Doing the founders proud
• Free to pray in school

- Environmental policy now much more an "option," less "necessary."
- President Because: Wanted To Be
- He's a good man, he said so in his ad
- Sued to block actual vote count
- Down with Bush / Up with Trees
- Design your own damn clothes!
- Just Don't Do It!
- Kill Bush / Save Trees
- Fuck you and your Free Trade
- Ask not what you can do for your country, ask what Bush is doing to your country
- Hoover never looked so compassionate
- As elusive as Sasquatch, the Compassionate Conservative
- This is truly the climate we have feared. Here it is.
- Declare a state of justice
- It's so sad to love cash
- Be American: Dissent
- Permanent Cultural Vibration
- Freedom for All
- Dear World Bank: Free People Not Markets

Archive #2: Debunker Mentality

DEBUNKER MENTALITY

Immediately following 9/11, NYC poets gathered in bars like everyone else, to drink and discuss, to not drink alone. Out of those melancholic encounters, the question was always, what should we do? Out of that question came Debunker Mentality, a group of volatile personalities who met weekly and on email to sloganize, design flyers, lexicons, and otherwise discuss the potential for language in the midst of language's co-option. We had just been told to "return to normal." We decided that instead, we needed to wheatpaste poems all over the city, to remind people of their primary HUMAN reaction to the Fallen Towers Atrocity. Called Poems of Grief, the following poems were distributed and wheatpasted around NYC for four consecutive weeks, beginning September 18, 2001:

- *Tree of Fire* by Adonis
- from: *Of Being Numerous* by George Oppen
- *Children of the Epoch* and *Any Case* by Wislawa Szymborska
- from: *Dictée* by Theresa Hak Kyung Cha
- *Conclusivity* by Fanny Howe
- *Wild honey has the scent of freedom* by Anna Akhmatova
- *M-Day's Child Is Fair of Face* by Muriel Rukeyser
- *My Time* by Osip Mandelshtam
- *The God of War* by B. Brecht
- *I know you, you are the deeply bowed* by Paul Celan
- *The Angel of History* passage by Walter Benjamin
- *Pride* by Dahlia Ravikovitch
- from: *Words in the Mourning Time* by Robert Hayden

FROM: WORDS IN THE
MOURNING TIME
by Robert Hayden

Oh, what a world we make.
oppressor and oppressed.

Our world—
this violent ghetto, slum
of the spirit raging against
itself.

We hate kill destroy
in the name of human good
our killing and our hate
destroy.

Debunker Mentality also created the following slogans, which were reproduced on posters for the 2001-2002 anti-war rallies:
• Ecrasez L'Infame (Crush the Infamy)
• Lose the Illusion of Your Exemption
• Mourn War
• We were always a part of history
• Refuse to Return to Normal
• Distrust the Men in Power
• The Bushes are Not Your Friends (But the Trees Are)

Archive #3: Document On Sloganizing

The following document was a letter from Rodrigo Toscano to Debunker Mentality, September 21, 2001. Moved by its relevance, I've inserted myself into the letter as a means of carrying on the conversation now, six years later.

That slogans preserve the moment somehow.

(That slogans date language?)

That however right we may be about the content leading up to that moment, we are not a mini-lecture series on wheels.

(The content of the moment is the act of being continuously present.)

That the slogans leave room enough for what might happen next.

(The future is only as long as the distance it takes for a slogan to actually have some effect.)

That they be adaptable enough to adjust if needed.

(Malleable Form.)

That slogans draw people out.

(By encouraging them to write their own slogans.)

That encourage them to stand up and join in.

(Amazing how many people at a political rally stop to comment on homemade signs that come from the heart.)

Homemade = up with people.

(That energize the converted.)

That signal the difficulty in doing so.

(The difficulty in being out here, no centrist compromise.)

Slogans that don't push us away from others.

(Sometimes even the people that act hostile toward us.)

That the affect, the gesture, and the content should be carefully examined in the interest of appeal, thoughtfulness, or sudden (ideo-effective) surprise.

(To subvert the very nature of sloganizing, to be self-reflective of the fact that one is a creator of propaganda.)

In a language that's easy to understand.

(Or not. We were barred from walking through the Vietnam Memorial in DC because our sign read: Freedom Is Relative. I'm still not exactly sure what that means, but the guards didn't care – because it was on a sign, it was a political message.)

"No Justice, No Peace." It should be fairly obvious to us here that however apt the slogan has been for other struggles (and very worthy ones at that), is not apt here at all.

(So the slogan must be vague enough to be timeless, but specific enough to be reflective of the current struggle.)

So with many other slogans. We should examine them for maximum effectively.

(Effectivity = non-isolation, non-isolating, non-stasis.)

We're not trying to re-convince ourselves (for the umpteenth time) of many of the principles we believe in and sometimes (though imperfectly) live by.

(We're not trying to state our superiority over all other apathetic life-forms. We are equally apathetic fleas on the machine.)

In fact, we're not "a we."

(Are you?)

Ever yet, but a dynamic (in process) Burgeoning Consensus against Death and Violence in all its forms.

(Except Duende, which we accept as a primal contradiction.)

Things we are having to defend ourselves about (already):

1. That, we are "do nothings"
    (Men In Suits shout: Get a Real Job! We reply: Hey, that's a great slogan! [under breath] *Asshole*.)

2. That we are relics of the 1960s.
    (Slogans like "declare peace" seal the deal. It is a justifiable thing to say and feel. But it seems too broad for the moment [a point of discussion], as well as being anchored by a "practical" eternity of some kind. Not everybody out there [unfortunately] is a peacenik [yet]. [I'd say problem of Ideological Transport Potential.])

3. That, we (as demonstrators) are "the same people as always (out there), the (supposed or alleged) "usual suspects'" and that we are "out of touch" somehow with the current mood of the nation (or even the polis).
    (And sometimes, we are. Was it justifiable to protest two days after 9/11, the city smelling of fire, bodies, paper? The policemen fatigued and in tears? And what were we protesting? The invasion that had not yet come to be... was this really the moment for that?)

4. That we are confused as to "The Message"
    (A slogan I penned off-the-cuff at Times Square: "For a lasting and
    (just) peace, the other ground zero." This might be a clumsily worded
    slogan, but perhaps it contains the elements of an equitable idea /
    practice (that preserves the moment). In short, it needs work.

As technicians of the word — poets, and cultural workers in general
    — we very much can and should enter into this burgeoning peace
    (justice) movement, to help shape it, and transform it. As living
    preceptors of now twisted truths, we must keep the political
    dialogue going, even though the politics of the moment seemingly
    lack the urgency of the politics of the past. There is always a-
    politics, a-language, a-idea that is on the waning side of articulation,
    unintelligible until dared to come into language.

Rodrigo Toscano to Debunker Mentality 09/01.
Reflected Insertions, Kristin Prevallet to Rodrigo Toscano, 01/06.

Archive #4: Lexicons

The lexicon project was conceived by Frances Richard and *Cabinet* Magazine. The idea was to reclaim words being used in the mass media by writing through their surface and into their deeper meanings.

NORMALCY:

NORM from *norma* meaning "the carpenter's square" meaning "a perpendicular line" meaning "knowing the time by looking at the sundial." What is the other side of the norm? The moondial which is witches time. Or: "The wish for normality is the other side of indifference" (*Yitzhak Laor*). So the other side of indifference is from the Greek word *gnomon* meaning "column or pin on a sundial that casts a shadow indicating time of day." The NORM is to always know the precise time of day. The time of day is read by perpendicular lines. (LOOK AT YOUR WATCH.) The other side of precision is indifference. So "not normal" means being disoriented, not knowing the precise time of day. "Return to normalcy" means "remain indifferent." *Regarding indifference*: "The brute fact is that (during wartime) daily life in the United States will not change significantly. Churches may be a little more crowded and airplanes a little less." *Regarding the current economy*: "'Normalcy' has been yanked out, we all find ourselves in an environment that, while similar on the surface, is based on an entirely new set of rules." *Regarding astrology:* The approach of the 12th planet has created confusion in Earth's magnetic field. The Earth's return to a normal magnetic field state will be delayed by several years. During the time of this passage, compasses will behave erratically. *Regarding the rest of the world:* "War and insecurity are the norm." *Regarding fascism:* "Voice or no voice the people can always be brought to the bidding of the leaders. All you have to do is tell them they are being attacked, and denounce the pacifists for lack of patriotism and exposing the country to danger (*Hermann Goering*)." All you have to do is change people's conception of time as no longer secure. Any minute (YOU COULD BE SHOPPING) you will be attacked. Any minute (YOU COULD HAVE ON THE WRONG SHOES) a biological weapon will cast a dark cloud over your city. When (NOT IF) this happens, time will stand still. *Regarding time:* "Mathematics held sway as French revolutionaries embarked on a project, to regulate time." To regulate time enforce the regulation of time. If you're not on our time, you're not normal. (LOOK AT YOUR WATCH). *Regarding utopia*: "Implicit in the pursuit of a society where everyone's lot is made the same through standardized repetition. This is the abolition of all elsewheres; of all difference." Abolish elsewhere. *Regarding a man talking on his cell phone on the train:* "We do all the work so that over there (A.K.A. THE MIDDLE EAST) they can live in their little dreamlands." *Regarding dreamland:* Over there, they refuse modernization. Meaning they refuse to measure time using our logic (SHOPPING). They have run out of time. Declaration 1441 makes it clear that they had enough time to disarm. They play games. Always scheming for more time. *Regarding bombing them:* "Now is the time for the council to tell him that the clock has not been stopped by his stratagems and his machinations (*Colin Powell*)." Keeping time while bombing them. "Freeing people by killing them? (*Robert Hayden*)." If time is so crucial, then drop watches, not bombs.

FORCE:

SCIENCE: between two bodies, the pull, dependent on the size of each. The presence that effects stillness, eliciting a change in motion ["Every body continues in its state of rest, or of uniform motion...unless it is compelled to change that state by forces impressed upon it." *Newton, Law 1, from Principia.*]; METAPHYSICS: The Pull which is unseen and just is; a power, a control, which has no origin and yet is everywhere ["May the force be with you."]; WAR: Strength in numbers, a body of armed men and women directed in their purpose ["The forces advanced through the jungle and fired upon all moving things, whether they be men or beasts"]; LAW: unlawful violence, to overpower without notions of restraint, reason ["He forced the gun into her side and held her face down at gunpoint"]; EMOTION: When a body is taken, overcome, possessed, rendered speechless by an enabling pull which seems to originate from somewhere outside of that body (see also, *science, metaphysics*) ["The force of his gaze stunned me. I wanted him to go towards him, and yet I could not move."]

The word force in and of itself does not include a sense of *measure*; i.e., used on its own, it assumes total and complete power over another body. In the case of a "forced entry," for example (the use of violence to clear a passageway, either through a doorway, or through a woman) there is absolutely no sense of measure: the entry was completely and absolutely cleared of its obstruction. However, in times of crisis, the word force is often used in conjunction either with the word *appropriate* or with the word *excessive*. APPROPRIATE FORCE implies that The Force has been tamed, its complete and total power over other bodies checked and balanced, its ability to cause motion in an inert body, stopped. In determining what *appropriate* force might be, there is the implication that the president and the military must be strategic, have many meetings, and carefully plot the implementation of force, firearms, or armed forces. Therefore, *appropriate* force is thoughtful, premeditated force. *Excessive* force, on the other hand, is the opposite: it is emotional, immediate, careless, and lacks restraint; it disregards Newton who said that force is relative to the size of each body. Although the word force may be balanced on the one side by what is *appropriate*, and on the other by what is *excessive*, when force is set into motion, when the nightstick has been raised, the gun fired, the punch made contact, the missile launched, what is the guiding principal determining if its actual execution is either *appropriate* or *excessive*? The answer: The actual implementation of force, set in motion, is neither *excessive*, nor *appropriate*. It is force, plain and simple. A word that when not modified by adjectives, sets into motion a potentially never-ending cycle of violence.

The Economy of Poetry
(Following Mark Lombardi's Web)

1.

This child plays with a plastic yellow bear
manufactured in Malaysia while this one
plays with a doll that was hand knit by her
mother.

This woman buys an apple pie from
MacDonald's for $1.10 and this woman picks
apples from an orchard for .60c/hour.

This woman is a bank teller and handles on
average $20,000 per day, but on weekends she
clips coupons from the newspaper in order to
save .35c on her next purchase of trash bags.

This man dreams of owning his own sailboat
so that he can disappear and never be forced
to turn on a computer or answer the phone
again.

This man was laid off from his job of 25 years
as a software engineer, and he sits around all
day long dreaming of once again having his
own cubicle.

This man is a revolutionary leader in Northern India and has mobilized 2,000 farmers in his state to stand up against their landlords and refuse to pay rent because they work the land day in and day out for nothing.

This woman cleans pools for a rich man in the city but dreams of returning home to the country to raise chickens.

This woman in Southern Mexico grows her own beets and tries to sell them at the local marketplace, but no one buys them because at the supermarket it's cheaper to buy beets which have been imported from Texas.

This man has so much money that he has to hire an accountant to keep track of all the zeros.

This man has no savings except the pennies and nickels he collects in mason jars under his sink.

This girl dreams of going to college to be a
doctor but knows her father can't afford it,
and so becomes a home health care worker
instead.

This woman is very old and can afford full-
time medical care, but she can't find anyone
to stay for longer than a few days because she
accuses anyone who comes into her house of
stealing her money.

This woman and this girl are all part of the
same economy—the one which confuses,
the one which distributes, the one which
subtracts, and the one which bleeds.

This is the difficulty of poetry.

2.

This man is a gangster who switched to union
busting when selling liquor became legal.

This is a man who remembers making rye in
his bathtub and smuggling it across town to
the local pool hall in mason jars disguised as
his wife's canned peaches.

This is a man who works with dangerous
chemicals in a non-unionized company, who
developed a painful chronic cough but is
unable to get the company doctor to diagnose
his problem as anything more than a common
cold.

This is a woman who needs to have sex with
five different men a night in order to pay
off the man who is threatening to kill her
children.

This is a man who works for other men to
make sure that none of the girls try and make
off with extra cash.

This woman is a faithful follower of Jesus who shows her devotion to Catholic teachings by placing $10 in the donation basket as it passes her in the pew, who can't afford a lawn mower and her weeds are out of control, which makes her neighbors infuriated because her weeds are ruining their yards.

This man works at a bank and personally witnessed a transaction in which a large sum of cash from the Vatican Bank was handed over to a man who he was certain was a part of the mafia.

This man's job is to transfer suitcases from one safe deposit box to another.

This man is an expert at masking the trace of large sums of money deposited into banks all over the world at any given time, who learned to play golf when he was a boy, who visualizes the global financial network as a vast golf course with millions of balls zipping around in the air simultaneously, being teed off and then dropping, rolling around a bit and then stopping, landing in holes where they vanish long enough to be out of view, only to resurface, once again to be teed off and sent whizzing into another direction. He imagines this constant activity of balls-in-motion and it helps him to focus on his drive. He by no means is an excellent golf player but Nelson Rockefeller once commended him for his stride, a compliment which won his brother several important defense contracts.

This woman is the wife of a guerilla who has
been hiding in the mountains for the past
five years; she thinks of him and his struggles
with the military officials who control the
democratically elected government every time
she visits her sister, whose son was murdered
just because he told the local police about a
white man from Miami who tried to convince
him to sell cocaine to the boys hanging out in
the schoolyard.

This is a man who loads airplanes destined to
Iraq with large crates which he knows contain
missiles, who buys his son a plastic machine
gun on the way home from work, who is a
devoted Lutheran and brilliant at barbecue
because he is very generous with the sauce.

This man is in the "destabilizing business"
and has made a huge profit selling missiles,
canons, and artillery to anti-rebel factions
within numerous third world countries; who
after the wars are won will then turn around
and sell the same weapons to the other side,
and so on and so on, until, he chuckles, they
finally "blow themselves off the face of the
earth."

This woman cannot understand why the
local hospital was bombed to bits by the
Americans.

This woman is weaving a large tapestry in
which a viscous circle of interconnecting lines
forms two scythes, and she imagines sewing
the point in which they meet as a singular
red dot, symbolizing her family which was
hacked to pieces because her brother dared to
give a wounded rebel fighter a ride to the local
hospital.

This man has picked up a machine gun and
vows to fire in the fight to save his country
until he is killed.

This man has successfully bribed another man
and therefore will not have to kill his family.

This man is terrified that a nuclear bomb
has fallen into the wrong hands, and worries
about his own personal safety.

This woman and this man are all connected to
the same network, the one that conceals, the
one that builds, the one that explodes and the
one that profits. Each thinks that he or she is
an independent entity, floating in a circular
bubble high above the concerns of politics and
economy.

No one can escape being implicated in the
flow: this is the difficulty of poetry.

Appendix:

Re: Shadow Poems
A shadow poem is a poem written in the shadow of another poem. There are many ways to write a shadow poem: 1) read a poem out loud, close the book, and then re-write the poem from memory. 2) follow the form of a poem, but change the content. 3) write in the tone of a poem, trying to write lines that the original poet could have written. 4) go line by line, writing the opposite of the line, or writing the same line, but with different language. 5) follow the rhyme scheme or measure of a poem, but change the content. 6) etc.

Re: Shadow Evidence Intelligence
These images are manipulations of three satellite "photographs" taken from Colin Powell's presentation to the United Nations, February 5, 2003, which were used to justify the invasion of Iraq. I was struck by how the photographs were decorated with arrows pointing to various fuzzy images, each with a designating word that supposedly "described" the image. Considering that someone obviously did all of this in Photoshop, I decided it wouldn't be out of line to do my own Photoshop rendering. The images were posted on CNN, which is where I initially captured them.

Re: The PIPA archives
The PIPA archives are indebted to the ideas of a wide group of poets, including:
David Stoler, Nicole Cooley, Lisa Birman, Marcella Durand, Lisa Jarnot, Rod Smith, Derek Fenner, David Michalski, Dave Friedman, jf, Joseph Torra, Tanya, Magdelana Zurawski, Frances Richard, Caroline Crumpacker, Anselm Berrigan, Karen Weiser, Tonya Foster, Susan Swensen, Rodrigo Toscano, Laura Elrick, Betsy Andrews, Rachel Levitsky, Alan Gilbert, Kristin Prevallet, Mónica de la Torre, Bruce Pearson, Alissa Quart, Allison Cobb, Jennifer Colman, Nathanial Siegel, David Cameron, Jules Boykoff, Kaia Sand... and that's only the beginning.

Re: Pop-Prop Agit and Spear Britney
As a conceptual poetry project, this work was abstracted from a poem that was written as rough notes documenting "where I was at": G-train, Brooklyn, NY, September 12, 2001, 2:45pm. At every stop, someone had radically defaced a series of ads for a Britney Spears Live from Las Vegas HBO concert. I wondered: were these violent inscriptions into a mass-media icon an action of displaced aggression or an articulation of fear;

were they covert activism (an "unpatriotic" rant) or just more graffiti? Regardless, subway riders were paying attention. They interacted with the posters by writing their own comments, and crossing out the comments that they disapproved of. I was very unsettled by these images. Haunted by the inscriptions. So, I wrote the following poem. A few weeks later, I discovered that the de(face)ment of Britney was the work of an artist named Debra Jenks.

"FAKE": BECAUSE PERFECTION LIKE WAR IS INHUMAN.
De-faces of Britney –
        Celebrity Mask –
                Displaced dissent in the reign of terror
scan&design with big blocky fonts, i.e. Blast—intersperse photos in
    between
(Missing: Feminist critics re: violence to women in times of war
    [check: A. Notley mentions this in her Homer talk?])
News Battery? (Beuys' bound yellowed newspaper stacks at Tate)
Photoshop—rub out certain parts of text and re-write over it.
Finish zap book news battery project.
Impressions:
The constant replay of falling towers.
Britney in an Elvis suit, flat chest, ripple of little breasts.
A photograph perfectly inhuman.
"FAKE."
This has got to be most defaced subway ad I have ever seen.
She has absorbed the anger, fear, confusion of NYC, September 2001.
Critique of media, capitalism, in time when the flags are raging on
    every corner.
Symbol of American Dream no longer possible.
A taunting reminder of how things used to be.
We hadn't yet been told to "return to normal."
Her face, a sign of backwards normalcy.
They had some displaced aggression.
To take out against the image.
The event, already saturated, over-represented.
Displaced aggression against it.
It was not the isolated event of these photos.
(As if they could be separated

from the immediate context
of fear and anticipation that surrounded them.)
Pop-star or super freak?
Interchangeable.
Celebrity face: mask upon which society writes its own meaning
    (Barthes).
Her androgyny meant she could be anything.
The blank slate.
She had to be punished.
They seem upset that her chest is flat.
Her chest being flat evokes child pornography.
"Don't let this happen to your little girl," one person writes.
"Fuck me please," another writes.
"One more time."
"She is not fake."
"Hollywood… don't believe the hype."
"Anyone can be a star."
"~~Stop~~ Start Rape Culture."
(Something is written by one person that is then crossed out by
    another.)

> *The stain*
> *upon which reality revolves*
> *passes over into the real*
> *the mysterious detail*
> *that "sticks out"*
> *that does not "fit" into the symbolic network*
> *of reality and that, as such,*
> *indicates that "something is amiss."*
> *Slavoj Zizek*

What was crossed out?
Public dialogue,
Back and forth out of tension,
Another epistolary tradition.
Awareness of analyzing needs to move beyond
        the image itself
            and into the intention
                behind it. Images are
                    not accidental, they are
                        designed and directed

                                        to catch the eye
                    of the passer-by.
                                    "Displaced aggression,"
                        Britney or HBO
                                        are not at this moment
                            so powerful,
                    they are now open to defacement.
Symbolic intent misdirected.
Analyzing the image
            should not refuse the politics
                    behind the defacement.
                    A sign is made,
                            a gesture brought
                                    into the light that
                                        obliterates the ability
            to think outside of it.
All of it is suspect
at some level.

The defacement
        of Britney
                is not a political gesture,
                        but it is an act of defiance:
                                dissent.
Displacement of
anger away from
            the actual source
                    of power that is causing
                        the pain, directed against
                                other objects—creating signs,
                                        codes that then

point to a larger critique.

(When in a regime any critique of government is considered suspect,
critique must necessarily be displaced:

not by trying to directly confront an issue but rather by moving
around it, coming at it from a different angle that is still pointed, but
not immediately recognizable.)

The left has for too long
cried "fascism"
and now the cry
isn't heard and the wolf
is upon us—

The sad face of Britney
                    bound and gagged
                        fucked and cut open
                            all the possible acts
                                of violence that can
                                    be done to a woman,
                                    knifed
                                    raped
                            crime rates are down
                                        says Michael Moore,
                                                    but

crimes against women

are up, says The New York Times.

Check. Regime is largely financed by
powerful military-industrial complex
and wealthy big business? Check.
Regime is xenophobic and
propaganda-obsessed and the
"Homeland/Fatherland"
is glorified beyond all others?
Check. Double Check.
Wake up. Check.

The future choice is whether to buy and consume anything at all.
Swallow up the entire cosmos
Replace one pious multiplex
       Where   you   are   nowhere:
                   you   are,   are you?

Re: Oil Oil Oil

This poem was generated using an Oulipo technique re-introduced by Juliana Spahr in the anthology *100 Days: An Anthology* edited by Andrea Brady and Keston Sutherland (Barque, 2001). The technique involves counting and eliminating certain words based on chance. I eliminated every seventh word in stanza #2, every sixth word in stanza #3, until the end of the poem when every other word was eliminated. It's possible that the final poem does not conform exactly to the constraints I just described: consistency may not be my strong-suit.

Re: The Economy of Poetry

This poem began as a response to The People Database, a project by the Belgian artist Annemie Maes, who rescued passport photographs from the trash of photo booths and scanned them into her computer, revealing weird chemical effects. See: www.unamas-projects.org/peopledatabase. The poem then evolved to another level when Susan Swensen invited me to contribute to a special issue of Pierogi Press devoted to the work of artist Mark Lombardi, who creates vast rhizomic diagrams of corporate and economic flow. See: www.pierogi2000.com/flatfile/lombardi.html for examples of his stunning work.